Main-Dish Grains

Little Vegetarian Feasts

Main-Dish Grains

Martha Rose Shulman

Author of *Little Vegetarian Feasts: Main-Dish Tarts and Gratins*

Illustrations by Debbie Drechsler

Bantam Books

NEW YORK   TORONTO   LONDON   SYDNEY   AUCKLAND

Little Vegetarian Feasts
Main-Dish Grains
A Bantam Book/June 1993

Library of Congress Cataloging-in-Publication Data

Shulman, Martha Rose.
Little vegetarian feasts. Main-dish grains/Martha Rose Shulman.

p. cm.
ISBN 0-553-08798-3
1. Cookery (Cereals) 2. Vegetarian cookery. 3. Entrées (Cookery)
I. Title.
TX808.S58   1993

641.5′636—dc20   92-21022
                                                                  CIP

Published simultaneously in the United States and Canada

Printed in THE UNITED STATES OF AMERICA
0   9   8   7   6   5   4   3   2   1

Main-Dish Grains

Contents

Introduction

When I first became interested in vegetarian cooking, I set about to learn about grains. What a world I discovered! Every week I would experiment with a different type—first millet, then bulgur, wheatberries, then kasha. Each time I cooked a different grain I discovered a new nutty taste and chewy texture. It never occurred to me to miss meat, so exciting was this new array of foods.

Grains feed more of the world's population than any other type of food; they come alive in different ways, depending on the culinary tradition. Indian pilafs and Asian rice dishes surprise the palate with an array of fragrant and pungent spices. Italians have brought out the best in their chewy round-grained rice with savory, unctuous risottos, and they transform humble cornmeal into creamy polentas that can be topped with any number of sauces. North Africans have made a specialty of aromatic couscous dishes. All over the Mediterranean, we find rice in fragrant stuffed vegetables, soups, and stews. And over the centuries, savory kasha dishes have warmed Russians and Eastern Europeans throughout their long, cold winters.

Although grains, like rye and wheatberries, have long cooking times, most of these pantry staples are really secret convenience foods. Bulgur and couscous don't require cooking at all, just twenty minutes soaking (while you do something else), and millet and rice require thirty to forty minutes of unsupervised cooking. Some dishes, like polenta and risotto, do take supervised cooking (and you'll see how well invested this time is when you taste the dishes), but you'll have plenty to choose from here. Grains aren't fussy; they can often be cooked ahead of time and held in the refrigerator for a few days. And the leftovers of practically every dish in this collection can be added to salads. They make unbelievably delicious fillings for flat omelets like the Kasha and Vegetable Frittata on page 30, stretching one dinner into two.

Cooking Grains

Whole grains are easy to prepare, and some (bulgur and couscous) are convenient because they don't need cooking at all. One cup of raw grain makes 4 ½-cup servings.

Barley. Looks somewhat like rice, with a rounder, beige-colored grain; has a similar flavor but chewier texture. "Pearl" barley has had the tough outer hull removed. Use 1 part barley, 2½ parts water or stock, and ¼ teaspoon salt per cup of barley if you're using water. Follow directions for brown rice, but cook for 45 minutes, until the barley is tender.

Bulgur. A nutty cracked-wheat cereal that has been precooked, then dehydrated. It comes in fine and medium grinds. Use 1 part bulgur to 2 parts water or stock. Place the bulgur in a bowl and stir in ¼ teaspoon salt per cup of bulgur if you're using water. Bring the water or stock to a boil and pour it over the bulgur. Let sit until the liquid is absorbed and the bulgur is soft, about 20 minutes. Fluff with a fork. If any excess liquid remains, drain and squeeze the bulgur in a strainer.

Couscous (Instant). Technically, couscous is a pasta, made from the hard hearts of durum wheat, but it behaves like a grain. Creamy white, it has a delicate flavor and texture. Cooked, dehydrated (instant) couscous is packaged and sold in supermarkets and health food stores. Use 1 part couscous to 1½ parts water or stock.

Place the couscous in a bowl, add ¼ teaspoon salt per cup of couscous if you're using water, and pour on warm or tepid water or stock. Let sit for 10 to 15 minutes, fluffing every once in a while with a fork or rubbing between your fingers so that the couscous doesn't clump together.

Kasha. Kasha, or buckwheat groats, is the triangular grain of the buckwheat plant. It comes roasted and unroasted and has a rich, earthy flavor. Use 1 part kasha to 2 parts water or stock. Have the stock or water simmering. Heat a tablespoon of sunflower or canola oil in a heavy-bottomed saucepan over medium heat and add the kasha. Sauté, stirring, until the grains begin to smell toasty, about 1 to 2 minutes. Add the simmering water or stock and ¼ teaspoon salt per cup of kasha if you're using water. Bring back to a boil, reduce the heat, cover, and simmer for 20 to 30 minutes, until the kasha is cooked through but not mushy. Pour off any liquid that might remain in the saucepan once the kasha is tender.

Millet. Small, nutty round yellow grains. Use 1 part millet to 2½ parts water or stock. Have the stock or water simmering. Heat a tablespoon of sunflower or canola oil in a heavy-bottomed saucepan over medium heat and add the millet. Sauté, stirring, until the grains begin to smell toasty, about 1 to 2 minutes. Add the simmering liquid or stock and ¼ teaspoon salt per cup of millet if you're using water. Bring back to a boil, reduce the heat, cover, and simmer for 35 to 45 minutes, until the grains are tender.

Quinoa. A native of Peru, these round, light-colored grains have a delicate flavor and smooth texture when cooked. Use 1 part quinoa to 2 parts water or stock. Soak the quinoa in a bowl of cold water to cover for 5 minutes. Spoon off any little specks that rise to the top, then drain through a strainer and run under cold water for another few minutes to remove impurities. Place the water in a saucepan and bring to a boil. Add ¼ teaspoon salt per cup of quinoa and stir in the quinoa. Reduce the heat, cover, and simmer for 15 to 20 minutes or until just cooked through, al dente. Drain off any remaining water.

Rice, Arborio. Italian rice used in risottos. The grain is short and round, the texture chewy. See recipes for risottos on pages 19, 33, 35, 37 for cooking instructions.

Rice, Basmati. This fine-textured rice has a unique earthy fragrance. For each cup of rice, use 2 quarts water or stock. Wash the rice in several changes of water until the water runs clear. Bring the water or stock to a boil in a large pot. Add ¼ teaspoon salt per cup of rice and add the rice. Stir for about 30 seconds, bring the water back to a boil, and cook, uncovered, for 5 minutes or until just tender. Drain and shake the rice in a strainer or colander.

Rice, Brown. Use 1 part rice to 2 parts water or stock. Combine the rice and water or stock in a saucepan and bring to a boil. Add ¼ teaspoon salt per cup of rice if you're using water, reduce the heat, cover, and simmer for

35 to 40 minutes, until the liquid is absorbed. If some water remains, cook, uncovered, until the rice just begins to stick to the bottom of the pan.

Rice, White, Long- and Short-Grain. Use 1 part rice to 2 parts water or stock. In certain recipes the rice is rinsed until the water runs clear. Bring the water or stock to a boil, add ¼ teaspoon salt per cup of rice if you're using water, and add the rice. Bring to a second boil, reduce the heat, cover, and simmer for 15 to 20 minutes, until the rice is tender. If any liquid remains in the pot, pour it off through a strainer.

Wheatberries, Whole Rye, Triticale. These all look like dark-colored rice and have a chewy texture and hearty, earthy taste. Triticale is a hybrid made from wheat and rye. Use 1 part grain to 3 parts water or stock. Combine the grain and water or stock and bring to a boil. Add ¼ teaspoon salt per cup of grain if you're using water. Reduce the heat, cover, and simmer for 50 minutes to an hour, until the grains are cooked through. Remove from the heat and pour off any excess liquid.

Basic Stocks

GARLIC STOCK

Makes 7 cups

Even though there are two heads of garlic here, this stock is fragrant rather than pungent. It makes a good substitute for chicken stock.

> 2 quarts water
> 2 heads of garlic, cloves separated and
>   peeled (see note)
> a bouquet garni
> ½ teaspoon dried thyme
> 1 to 2 teaspoons salt (to taste)
> 6 peppercorns
> 1 tablespoon olive oil

Combine all the ingredients in a stockpot and bring to a boil. Cover, reduce the heat, and simmer for 1 to 2 hours. Strain and adjust the salt. This will keep for 3 or 4 days in the refrigerator and freezes well.

Note: To peel all the garlic cloves, hit them with the bottom of a jar or glass or lean on them with the flat side of a knife. The skins will pop off, and it doesn't matter if the garlic cloves are slightly crushed.

VeGeTaBLe STock

Here's a quick, simple vegetable stock to use in these recipes.

    2 quarts water
    2 large onions, quartered
    2 large carrots, coarsley sliced
    2 large leeks, cleaned and sliced
    3 garlic cloves, peeled
    2 celery ribs, with leaves, coarsely sliced
    a bouquet garni
    ½ pound (2 medium) potatoes, scrubbed
       and diced
    salt to taste
    1 teaspoon peppercorns

Combine all the ingredients in a stockpot and bring to a
boil. Reduce the heat, cover, and simmer for 1 to 2 hours.
Strain and discard the vegetables. This will keep for 4 days
in the refrigerator and freezes well.

Recipes

Pumpkin Risotto

Serves 6

The pumpkin melts into this sweet-tasting risotto as it cooks, giving it a lovely pale orange hue and a creamy texture.

> 7 cups vegetable or garlic stock (pages 16–17)
> 2 tablespoons olive oil
> ½ small onion or 1 shallot, minced
> 2 pounds fresh pumpkin, peeled and diced
> salt to taste
> 2 to 3 large garlic cloves to taste, minced or put through a press
> 1 teaspoon fresh thyme leaves or ½ teaspoon dried, or 2 tablespoons chopped fresh sage or 2 teaspoons dried
> pinch of freshly grated nutmeg
> 2 cups Italian Arborio rice, washed
> ½ cup dry white wine
> 1 large egg, beaten
> 2 ounces Parmesan cheese, grated (½ cup)
> freshly ground pepper to taste

1. Have the stock simmering in a saucepan.
2. Heat the oil in a large heavy-bottomed skillet over medium-low heat. Add the onion or shallot and sauté until the onion is tender and beginning to color, about 5 minutes. Add the pumpkin, a little salt, and the garlic and sauté for about 3 to 5 minutes, until the pumpkin is coated with oil and beginning to soften. Add the thyme or sage, nutmeg, ⟫→

19

and rice and continue to sauté, stirring, for a few minutes, until all the grains are separate.

3. Stir in the white wine and cook over medium heat, stirring constantly. The wine should bubble, but not too quickly. You want some of the flavor to cook into the rice before it evaporates.

4. When the wine has just about evaporated, stir in a ladleful or two of the stock. It should just cover the rice and should bubble slowly. Cook, stirring constantly, until it is just about absorbed. Add another ladleful of the stock and continue to cook in this fashion, adding more broth when the rice is almost dry. After 25 to 35 minutes the rice should be cooked al dente, firm to the bite.

5. Beat together the egg and the Parmesan. Add another ladleful of stock to the rice so that the rice is not completely dry; remove from the heat. Stir half a ladleful of stock into the egg and cheese mixture and immediately stir this into the rice. Combine well, taste, and adjust seasonings, adding salt and pepper as desired. Return to the heat and stir for a few seconds, then serve at once.

Millet and Cashew Pilaf

Millet has a delicate, nutty flavor all its own that is all the more evident when you combine it with cashews. Serve this subtly seasoned pilaf with a curried vegetable side dish.

- 2 tablespoons canola oil
- 6 green cardamom pods
- 1 cinnamon stick, 3 inches long
- 8 whole cloves
- 2 cups millet
- 5 cups simmering vegetable stock (page 17) or water
- ½ teaspoon salt (if using water)
- 1 teaspoon saffron threads
- ¼ cup currants, chopped dried apricots, or golden raisins
- ⅔ cup coarsely chopped raw cashews
- 1 medium onion, chopped
- 2 large garlic cloves, minced or put through a press
- 2 teaspoons grated or minced fresh ginger
- 2 large carrots, thinly sliced
- 1 to 1½ cups plain yogurt for topping

1. Heat 1 tablespoon of the oil in a heavy-bottomed saucepan over medium heat and add the spices. Cook for 1 minute and stir in the millet. Cook, stirring, for another minute or two, until the millet begins to smell toasty, then add the stock or water, salt, saffron, and dried fruit. When the stock or water comes back to a boil, reduce the heat, cover, and simmer 25 minutes, or until the millet is tender and the liquid absorbed

2. Meanwhile, roast the cashews in a dry frying pan or a moderate oven until lightly browned, stirring frequently. Set aside.

3. Heat the remaining oil in a heavy-bottomed nonstick skillet over medium heat and add the onion. Sauté, stirring often, for 5 minutes, or until the onion softens. Add the garlic, ginger, and carrots and continue to cook, stirring, for another 5 minutes, or until the carrots are crisp-tender. Add a couple of tablespoons of water if the vegetables begin to stick.

4. Stir in the cashews and the cooked millet and heat through. Adjust seasoning if necessary. Serve each portion with a generous dollop of yogurt.

Polenta with Tomato and Bean Sauce

The combination of beans and corn usually makes us think of Mexico, but this dish is decidedly Italian.

For the Tomato and Bean Sauce:
1 tablespoon olive oil
1 small onion, chopped
3 to 4 garlic cloves to taste, minced or put
   through a press
3 pounds fresh or drained canned tomatoes,
   peeled, seeded, and chopped
pinch of sugar
salt to taste
2 cups (1 14-ounce can) cooked borlotti or
   red kidney beans, drained (⅔ cup dried)
1 teaspoon chopped fresh or ½ teaspoon
   crumbled dried rosemary
freshly ground pepper to taste
2 tablespoons slivered fresh basil or
   chopped fresh parsley

For the Polenta:
6½ cups water
2 teaspoons unsalted butter
1¼ teaspoons salt
2 cups (¾ pound) coarse stone-ground
   yellow cornmeal
freshly ground black pepper

2 ounces Parmesan cheese, grated (½ cup)

1. First make the sauce. Heat the olive oil in a heavy-bottomed saucepan over medium-low heat and add the onion and one third of the garlic. Cook, stirring, until the onion is tender, then add the tomatoes, remaining garlic, sugar, and salt. Bring to a simmer and cook, uncovered, for 15 minutes, stirring often. Stir in the beans and rosemary, cover, and simmer for 5 minutes. Add the pepper and stir in the basil or parsley. Adjust garlic and salt. Remove from the heat and set aside.

2. Cook the polenta. Bring the water to a boil in a large pot and add the butter and salt. Turn the heat down to medium-low so that the water is boiling gently, a little faster than a simmer. Very slowly add the cornmeal, taking it up in handfuls and letting it run between your fingers in a very thin stream. Whisk the water constantly as you add the cornmeal. Now change to a long-handled wooden spoon and turn the heat down to low. Stir the polenta constantly with the wooden spoon over low heat until it thickens and is difficult to stir. It is done when it comes away from the sides of the pot. This should take about 20 minutes. Stir in some freshly ground pepper and remove from the heat.

3. Transfer the polenta to a warm platter or gratin dish and make a well in the center. Bring the sauce back to a simmer and pour it into the well. Sprinkle on the Parmesan and serve.

Lemony Bulgar and Chick-Pea Pilaf

This dish has everything I like about tabouli, the Middle
Eastern salad — bulgur, lemon, olive oil, and parsley. The
combination is just as wonderful in this hot version, which
adds cumin, green pepper, and chick-peas.

> 1 cup medium-grind bulgur
> 2 cups vegetable stock (page 17) or bouillon
> 1 teaspoon ground cumin (or more to taste)
> 1 tablespoon olive oil
> 1 small onion, chopped
> 1 small green bell pepper, chopped
> 2 to 3 large garlic cloves to taste, minced or
>   put through a press
> 2 cups cooked chick-peas (1 cup dried) or 1
>   14-ounce can, drained
> ⅓ cup fresh lemon juice
> 1 cup chopped fresh parsley
> salt and freshly ground pepper to taste

1. Place the bulgur in a bowl. Bring the stock to a boil, add half the cumin, and pour the stock over the bulgur. Stir once and let sit for 10 to 15 minutes, until most of the liquid has been absorbed and the bulgur is fluffy.

2. Heat the olive oil in a large heavy-bottomed skillet over medium heat and add the onion, green pepper, and half the garlic. Sauté, stirring, until the onion is translucent, about 3 to 5 minutes, then add the remaining garlic and cumin. Sauté for about 30 seconds, then stir in the bulgur and chick-peas. Stir together for a few minutes, then add the lemon juice and parsley. Combine well, add salt and pepper, and remove from the heat. Serve hot.

Barley and Mushroom Pilaf

Barley and mushrooms always make a great marriage. This savory pilaf is "meaty" and substantial.

> 1 ounce (1 cup) dried porcini
> boiling water to cover the porcini
> 3 cups vegetable stock (page 17) or bouillon
> 1 tablespoon olive oil
> 2 shallots, minced
> 1 pound mushrooms, thickly sliced
> 4 garlic cloves, minced or put through a
>   press
> 1 tablespoon soy sauce
> 1 teaspoon fresh thyme leaves or ½
>   teaspoon dried thyme
> 1 teaspoon chopped fresh rosemary or ½
>   teaspoon crumbled dried rosemary
> ½ cup dry white wine
> ½ pound (1 heaped cup) barley, rinsed
> salt and freshly ground pepper to taste

1. Place the dried mushrooms in a bowl and pour on boiling water. Let sit for 15 minutes, until the mushrooms are softened. Drain through a cheesecloth-lined strainer and add the liquid to the stock. Rinse the mushrooms in several changes of water and squeeze dry.

2. Bring the stock to a simmer in a saucepan.

3. In a large heavy-bottomed lidded skillet or Dutch oven, heat the olive oil over medium heat and add the shallots. Sauté until the shallots begin to color, about 5 minutes. Add the soaked porcini, sliced fresh mushrooms, and one quarter of the garlic. Sauté, stirring, until the mushrooms begin to release liquid, about 5 minutes, then add the remaining garlic, soy sauce, thyme, rosemary, and 2 tablespoons of the wine. Cook, stirring, until the mushrooms are softened and fragrant, 5 to 10 minutes, then stir in the barley. Stir over medium heat for about 30 seconds, then add the remaining wine. Cook, stirring, until the barley has absorbed the wine, then stir in the simmering stock and salt and pepper. When it comes to a second boil, reduce the heat, cover, and simmer over low heat for 30 to 40 minutes, until the liquid has been just about absorbed and the barley is tender. Remove from the heat, adjust seasonings, transfer to a serving dish or platter, and serve.

Kasha and Vegetable Frittata

Kasha has such a lovely rich flavor and goes very well in this savory, nutty omelet. The onions and peppers add sweetness and color. It's terrific cold and travels well in a lunchbox.

2 tablespoons olive oil
1 small onion, sliced
1 or 2 large garlic cloves to taste, minced
2 medium-size red bell peppers, sliced into thin strips
2 teaspoons balsamic vinegar
⅔ cup kasha, cooked (page 12)
salt and freshly ground pepper to taste
6 large eggs
¼ cup chopped fresh parsley

1. Heat 1 tablespoon of the olive oil in a large nonstick skillet over medium heat and add the onion, garlic, and red pepper. Sauté until the onion is tender and translucent, about 3 to 5 minutes. Add the vinegar and continue to sauté over medium heat until the vegetables are softened and beginning to brown, about 5 to 8 more minutes. Stir in the kasha, stir together for about a minute, add salt and pepper, and remove from the heat.

2. Beat the eggs with a whisk; stir in the vegetable/kasha mixture, parsley, and more salt and pepper if you wish.

3. Heat the remaining olive oil in a large nonstick skillet (use the same one you used for the onion and pepper) over medium-high heat and pour in the omelet mixture. Shake the pan vigorously for the first few seconds and lift the edges of the mixture with a spatula, allowing the egg to run underneath; then cover and turn down the heat to medium-low and let the omelet cook slowly until just about cooked through. Meanwhile, preheat the broiler.

4. When the omelet has set on the bottom and is just about cooked through, place the pan under the broiler and cook until the top is lightly browned. The entire cooking time shouldn't be more than about 10 minutes. Serve hot, at room temperature, or cold, cut into wedges.

Sweet Pepper Risotto

Serves 6

The Italians have developed a unique technique for cooking rice into a creamy mixture where each grain retains its chewy identity. This risotto is sweet, colorful, and luscious.

> 7 cups vegetable or garlic stock (pages 16–17)
> 2 tablespoons olive oil
> ½ small onion or 1 shallot, minced
> 3 large (1½ pounds) red bell peppers, cut into thin 1-inch-long strips
> salt to taste
> 2 to 3 large garlic cloves to taste, minced or put through a press
> 1 teaspoon fresh thyme leaves or ½ teaspoon dried
> 2 cups Italian Arborio rice, washed
> ½ cup dry white wine
> pinch of saffron threads
> 1 large egg, beaten
> 2 ounces Parmesan cheese, grated (½ cup)
> freshly ground pepper to taste

1. Have the stock simmering in a saucepan.
2. Heat the oil in a large heavy-bottomed skillet over medium-low heat. Add the onion or shallot and sauté until tender and beginning to color, about 5 minutes. Add the ⟫⟶

peppers, a little salt, and the garlic and sauté for about 3 to 5 minutes, until the peppers are coated with oil and beginning to soften. Add the thyme and rice and continue to sauté, stirring, until all the grains are separate, about 2 to 3 minutes.

3. Stir in the wine and cook over medium heat, stirring constantly. The wine should bubble, but not too quickly. You want some of the flavor to cook into the rice before it evaporates.

4. When the wine has just about evaporated, stir in a ladleful of the simmering stock and the saffron. The stock should just cover the rice and should bubble slowly. Cook, stirring constantly, until it is just about absorbed. Add another ladleful of the stock and continue to cook in this fashion, not too fast but not too slowly, adding more stock when the rice is almost dry. After 25 to 35 minutes the rice should be cooked al dente, firm to the bite.

5. Beat together the egg and the Parmesan. Add another ladleful of stock to the rice so that the rice is not completely dry; remove from the heat. Stir half a ladleful of stock into the egg and cheese mixture and immediately stir this into the rice. Combine well, taste, and adjust seasonings, adding salt and pepper. Return to the heat and stir for a few seconds, then serve at once.

Fennel Risotto

Fennel gives this risotto a sweet, slightly pungent flavor. The delicate leaves added at the end intensify the flavor.

> 7 cups vegetable or garlic stock (pages 16–17)
> 2 pounds fennel (2 medium bulbs), trimmed and chopped
> salt to taste
> 2 tablespoons olive oil
> ½ small onion or 1 shallot, minced
> 2 to 3 large garlic cloves, minced or put through a press
> 2 teaspoons fresh thyme leaves or 1 teaspoon dried
> 2 cups Italian Arborio rice, washed
> ½ cup dry white wine
> freshly ground pepper to taste
> 1 large egg, beaten
> 2 ounces Parmesan cheese, grated (½ cup)

1. Have the stock simmering in a saucepan. Chop the feathery leaves of the fennel and set aside. Discard the stalks.

2. Heat the oil in a large heavy-bottomed skillet over medium-low heat and sauté the onion or shallot until tender and beginning to color. Add the fennel, a little salt, and garlic and sauté for about 3 to 5 minutes, until the fennel is coated with oil and beginning to soften. Add the thyme and ⟫⟫⟶

the rice and continue to sauté, stirring, until all the grains are separate.

3. Stir in the wine and cook over medium heat, stirring all the while. The wine should bubble slowly.

4. When the wine has just about evaporated, stir in a ladleful of the stock. Cook, stirring constantly, while the stock bubbles slowly, until it is just about absorbed. Add another ladleful of the stock and continue to cook, adding more stock when the rice is almost dry. After 25 to 35 minutes the rice should be cooked al dente, firm to the bite.

5. Beat together the egg and the Parmesan. Add another ladleful of stock to the rice so that the rice is not completely dry; remove from the heat. Stir half a ladleful of stock into the egg and cheese mixture and immediately stir this into the rice, along with the chopped fennel leaves. Add salt and pepper to taste. Return to the heat and stir for a few seconds, then serve at once.

Radicchio Risotto

This slightly bitter risotto is a Venetian specialty. The radicchio gives the rice a purplish hue.

> 7 cups vegetable or garlic stock (pages 16–17)
> 2 tablespoons olive oil
> ½ small onion or 1 shallot, minced
> 1½ pounds radicchio, leaves washed and cut in thin strips (8 cups)
> salt to taste
> 3 to 4 large garlic cloves to taste, minced or put through a press
> 2 cups Italian Arborio rice, washed
> ½ cup dry white wine
> 1 large egg, beaten
> 2 ounces Parmesan cheese, grated (½ cup)
> ¼ cup chopped fresh parsley
> freshly ground pepper to taste

1. Have the stock simmering in a saucepan.

2. Heat the oil in a large heavy-bottomed skillet and sauté the onion or shallot over medium-low heat until the onion is tender and beginning to color. Add the radicchio, a little salt, and the garlic, and sauté for about 3 to 5 minutes, until the radicchio is wilted and coated with oil. Add the rice ≫➔

37

and continue to sauté, stirring, for a few minutes, until all the grains are separate.

3. Stir in the wine and cook over medium heat, stirring all the while. The wine should bubble slowly.

4. When the wine has just about evaporated, stir in a ladleful or two of the stock. It should just cover the rice and should bubble slowly like the wine. Cook, stirring constantly, until it is just about absorbed. Add another ladleful of the stock and continue stirring, adding more broth when the rice is almost dry. After 25 to 35 minutes the rice should be cooked al dente, firm to the bite.

5. Beat together the egg and the Parmesan. Add another ladleful of stock to the rice, so that the rice is not completely dry, and remove from the heat. Stir half a ladleful of stock into the egg and cheese mixture and immediately stir this into the rice, along with the parsley. Combine well, taste, and adjust seasonings, adding salt and pepper as desired. Return to the heat and stir for a few seconds, then serve at once.

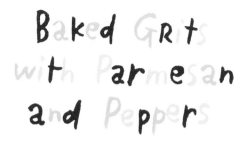

Baked Grits with Parmesan and Peppers

This dish is puddinglike: creamy, savory, and comforting.

5 cups water
salt to taste
1 cup grits
2 tablespoons olive oil
1 small onion, chopped
2 large garlic cloves, minced or put through
   a press
1 large green bell pepper, chopped
1 large red bell pepper, chopped
freshly ground pepper to taste
¼ pound Parmesan cheese, grated (1 cup)
1 large egg, beaten

1. Bring the water to a boil in a large saucepan. Add ¾ teaspoon salt and slowly stir in the grits. Cover, reduce the heat to low, and simmer for 20 minutes, stirring occasionally. Meanwhile, preheat the oven to 400 degrees and oil a 3-quart baking dish.

2. While the grits are cooking, heat 1 tablespoon of the oil in a large heavy-bottomed skillet over medium-low heat and add the onion. Cook, stirring, until the onion begins to ➤➤

soften, about 3 minutes. Add the garlic and peppers and cook, stirring often, for 5 minutes, until the peppers are crisp-tender. Add salt and pepper, cook for another minute or so, and remove from the heat.

3. Remove the grits from the heat and stir in all but 2 tablespoons of the cheese, then stir in the egg and the vegetables. Add salt and pepper to taste. Transfer to the oiled baking dish. Sprinkle the remaining cheese over the top and drizzle on the remaining oil. Bake for 15 to 20 minutes, until the top is light brown and crusty. Remove from the oven and serve.

Spicy Vegetable Couscous

Serves 6 to 8

You can vary the vegetables in this filling, piquant couscous according to the seasons. Use pumpkin or butternut squash in winter, zucchini in summer. Add green beans, peas, and corn in season.

1 tablespoon olive oil
1 large or 2 small onions, sliced
3 to 4 garlic cloves, minced or put through a
   press

½ pound dried chick-peas or white beans,
   washed, picked over, soaked overnight or
   for several hours, and drained
1 leek, white part only, cleaned and sliced
2 celery stalks, sliced
1 pound tomatoes, peeled and coarsely
   chopped, or 1 large can (28 ounces)
   tomatoes, drained
6 cups water
1 fresh jalapeño or other hot green chili,
   seeded and sliced
1 bay leaf
½ teaspoon saffron threads
¾ pound carrots, thickly sliced
¾ pound turnips, peeled and cut in wedges
salt and freshly ground pepper to taste
¾ pound zucchini, thickly sliced, or winter
   squash, diced
cayenne to taste
2 heaping cups instant couscous
½ cup water
1 bunch cilantro, chopped
For garnish: whole sprigs of cilantro
   harissa sauce

1. Heat the olive oil in a large heavy-bottomed stockpot.
Add the onion and half the garlic and sauté until the onion
begins to soften. Add the beans, leek, celery, tomatoes,
water, hot green chili, and bay leaf and bring to a boil.
Reduce the heat, cover, and simmer 1 hour.
2. Add the saffron, remaining garlic, carrots, turnips, salt,
and pepper. Cover and simmer another hour. Add the zucchini or winter squash and cayenne to taste. Simmer for ⟫⟶

another half hour, or until the squash is tender. Adjust seasonings.

3. Place the couscous in a large bowl or a casserole. Combine 2 cups broth from the vegetable mixture and ½ cup water. Gradually sprinkle this onto the couscous. Add more water if the couscous isn't covered. Let the couscous sit for 20 minutes and stir with a wooden spoon or between your palms and fingers every 5 minutes or so to prevent it from clumping. It should swell and soften. Add salt to taste.

4. Heat the reconstituted couscous through for 15 to 20 minutes in a strainer or steamer that fits tightly over your soup pot, or in an oiled baking dish in a medium oven (drizzle a tablespoon of olive oil over the top).

5. Just before serving, bring the vegetable mixture back to a simmer and stir in the chopped cilantro. To serve, spoon the couscous into warmed wide, flat soup bowls and ladle on a generous helping of the soup with lots of vegetables. Garnish with sprigs of cilantro. Pass the harissa along with a small bowl of broth so that people can dissolve the spicy harissa in a spoonful before adding it to the couscous.

Iranian Rice and Vegetable Pilaf

Serves 6 to 8

Rice cooked in yogurt? This golden-crusted, festive dish—a vegetarian version of a traditional Iranian meat and rice dish—may seem rather strange to you, but you won't think so when you taste it. It works best if cooked in a heavy-bottomed nonstick skillet. You can use a pizza pan for a lid.

1 pound Carolina long-grain rice (2¼ cups)
1 medium-size eggplant, cut in half lengthwise
2 tablespoons canola or olive oil
2 medium onions
4 garlic cloves, peeled and left whole
1 large red bell pepper, chopped
¼ cup pine nuts
¼ cup currants
2 medium-size zucchini, sliced about ¼ inch thick
1 tablespoon balsamic vinegar
3 medium-size tomatoes, peeled, seeded, and chopped
½ cup water
salt and freshly ground pepper to taste
4 quarts water
2 teaspoons additional salt for the rice
3½ cups plain yogurt
1 teaspoon powdered saffron

≫→

1. Place the rice in a colander and place the colander in a bowl under running water. Rinse while you prepare the vegetables.

2. Preheat the oven to 475 degrees. Score the eggplant down the cut side, being careful not to cut through the skin. Place cut side down on a lightly oiled baking sheet and bake in the oven for 20 minutes, or until the skin is shriveled. Remove from the heat, allow to cool, and dice.

3. Make the vegetable ragout. Heat 1 tablespoon of the oil in a large heavy-bottomed nonstick skillet and add the onions. Sauté until tender, about 5 minutes, and add 1 garlic clove, the red pepper, and a large pinch of salt. Cook, stirring, over medium-low heat, for about 5 minutes.

4. Add the eggplant, remaining garlic, pine nuts, currants, and zucchini. Cook, stirring, for a minute or two and stir in the vinegar, tomatoes, ½ cup water, and salt and pepper to taste. Continue to cook, stirring often, for 25 to 30 minutes, or until the vegetables are tender and fragrant. Transfer to a bowl. Adjust seasonings.

5. Place the water in a large pot and bring to a boil over a high flame. Drain the rice and add to the water, along with 2 teaspoons salt. As soon as the water comes back to a boil, drain the rice and rinse again.

6. Mix together 2 cups of the yogurt and the saffron. Heat the remaining oil in a large heavy-bottomed nonstick skillet and add the yogurt-saffron mixture and salt to taste. Spread it over the bottom of the pan, and when it begins to bubble, add the rice. Using the back of a spoon, make a depression in the middle of the rice and add the vegetables in an even layer. Cover tightly, reduce heat to very low, and cook for 25 minutes, or until the rice is just beginning to stick to the bottom of the pan. Remove from the heat and let sit for a minute or two.

7. Gently loosen the rice with a spatula. Place a platter over the top of the pan and reverse the pilaf onto the platter. If the rice sticks, just scrape it off with a spatula and lay over the top. Serve, passing the remaining yogurt in a bowl.

Gingery Stir-Fried Rice, Tofu, and Vegetables

Serves 6

This is a wonderful way to recycle leftover cooked rice.

2 tablespoons canola, sunflower, or
  safflower oil
1 onion, sliced
2 carrots, thinly sliced on the diagonal
2 large garlic cloves, minced or put through
  a press
1 tablespoon chopped fresh ginger
½ pound (2 squares) firm tofu, diced
2 tablespoons tamari or Kikkoman soy
  sauce (or more to taste)
1 bunch broccoli, broken into florets
¼ cup water
3 cups cooked brown rice (1½ cups
  uncooked)
2 large eggs, beaten
2 to 3 tablespoons chopped cilantro to taste

1. Heat 1 tablespoon of the oil in a large heavy-bottomed skillet or wok over medium heat and add the onion and carrots. Sauté, stirring, until the onion is translucent, 3 to 5 minutes, then add the garlic and ginger. Sauté for about 30 seconds, just until the garlic begins to color, and add the tofu. Sauté, stirring, for about 3 minutes, until the tofu begins to color, and add the soy sauce. When the soy sauce has been absorbed by the tofu, add the broccoli, stir ➤

47

together, and add the water. Cook, stirring, for 5 minutes, or until the broccoli is crisp-tender and the water has evaporated.

2. Add the remaining oil and the rice. Cook, stirring, until the rice is heated through and beginning to toast. Stir in the eggs and cilantro, add more soy sauce if desired, and as soon as the eggs are cooked through, after about 1 minute, remove from the heat and serve.

Sweet and Sour Red Cabbage with Bulgur

Serves 4 to 6

This sweet and pungent combination is a classic. The cabbage would go equally well with other nutty grains such as quinoa or kasha.

> 1½ cups fine- or medium-grain bulgur
> ½ teaspoon salt
> 2 cups boiling water
> 2 tart apples, peeled if waxed, cored, and sliced
> 1 tablespoon fresh lemon juice
> 3 tablespoons cider or red wine vinegar
> 2 tablespoons mild-flavored honey
> ½ cup apple juice
> ½ cup water
> 2 tablespoons canola oil
> 2 medium onions, sliced

½ teaspoon ground cloves
½ teaspoon ground allspice
1 teaspoon ground cinnamon
1 pound red cabbage, cored and shredded
  (about 4 cups)
salt to taste
2 tablespoons raisins
freshly ground pepper to taste
1 cup plain low-fat yogurt
12 toasted almonds, ground

1. Place the bulgur in a 2-quart casserole, mix with the salt, and pour on the boiling water. Set aside.

2. Toss together the apples and lemon juice. Stir together the vinegar, honey, apple juice, and water.

3. Heat 1 tablespoon of the oil in a large heavy-bottomed nonstick skillet over medium-low heat and add the onions. Cook, stirring, for about 10 minutes, until they begin to color. Add the spices, stir together for about a minute, and add the remaining oil, the cabbage, and about ¼ teaspoon salt. Stir together for a few minutes, until the cabbage is just beginning to wilt, and add the raisins, apples, and vinegar mixture.

4. Cook over medium-low heat, stirring often, for 30 to 40 minutes, adding water if necessary, until the cabbage is tender and the mixture fragrant. Adjust salt, add pepper, and remove from the heat.

5. Place the bulgur in a strainer and press out any excess water. Transfer to a warm serving dish or platter. Top with the sweet and sour cabbage and spoon the yogurt over the top. Sprinkle with the almonds and serve.

Vegetable Paella

Serves 6 to 8

I've had vegetarians ask me if I was sure there was no fish in this paella. I'm not sure why they're suspicious; perhaps the saffron makes this reminiscent of seafood paellas.

6 cups vegetable or garlic stock (pages 16–17)
2 tablespoons olive oil
2 medium onions, chopped
4 large garlic cloves, minced or put through a press
1 green bell pepper, sliced
1 red bell pepper, sliced
salt to taste
1 pound (4 medium-size) tomatoes, peeled and chopped
freshly ground pepper to taste
1 teaspoon paprika
2 cups Carolina, Italian Arborio, or Valencia rice
½ cup dry white wine
1 teaspoon saffron (either threads or ground)
½ pound green beans, trimmed and cut in 1-inch lengths (2 cups)
2 cups cooked chick-peas (1 cup raw, or 1 14-ounce can)
1 cup fresh peas or ¼ pound more green beans
½ cup imported black olives, for garnish

1. Have the stock simmering in a saucepan.

2. Heat 1 tablespoon of the oil over medium heat in a large heavy-bottomed nonstick skillet, wok, or paella pan. Add the onions and cook, stirring, for 3 minutes, until they begin to soften. Add half the garlic, the peppers, and a large pinch of salt and continue to cook, stirring, until the onion is beginning to color and the peppers are tender, about 5 to 10 minutes. Add the tomatoes, some pepper, and the paprika and sauté, stirring often, for about 5 minutes.

3. Add the remaining tablespoon of oil and the rice. Stir together for a couple of minutes and add the wine. Stir until the wine has evaporated and add the stock, salt if necessary, pepper, and saffron. Turn the heat to medium-low and simmer 10 minutes, stirring occasionally. Add the green beans, chick-peas, and fresh peas. Simmer another 15 to 20 minutes, stirring occasionally, or until the stock is absorbed and the beans are tender. Taste and adjust seasonings. Garnish with black olives and serve.

Savory Wheatberry Pilaf

The wheatberries in this fragrant, heavenly pilaf have a
marvelous chewy texture and a rich, satisfying taste.

> ½ ounce (½ cup) dried porcini
> boiling water to cover the porcini
> 3½ cups vegetable stock (page 17)
> 1 tablespoon olive oil
> 1 small onion, minced
> 2 garlic cloves, minced or put through a
>   press
> 1 carrot, diced
> 1 celery rib, diced
> ½ pound (1 heaped cup) whole
>   wheatberries, rinsed
> ½ cup dry white wine or beer
> ½ bunch (¾ pound) broccoli, broken into
>   florets (2 cups)
> ½ teaspoon dried thyme
> 2 tablespoons chopped fresh parsley
> salt and freshly ground pepper to taste
> 1 ounce Parmesan cheese, grated (¼ cup)

1. Place the porcini in a bowl and pour on boiling water. Let
sit for 15 minutes, until the mushrooms are softened. Drain
through a cheesecloth-lined strainer. Add the soaking
liquid to the stock. Rinse the mushrooms in several changes
of water and squeeze dry. Chop coarsely and set aside.

2. Bring the stock to a simmer in a saucepan.

3. Heat the oil in a large heavy-bottomed lidded skillet or

Dutch oven over medium-low heat and add the onion and half the garlic. Cook, stirring, until the onion begins to soften, about 3 minutes, then add the carrot and celery. Cook, stirring, for 5 minutes. Add the wheatberries, chopped porcini, and remaining garlic, stir together for another minute or two, and add the wine or beer. Cook, stirring, over medium-low heat for a couple of minutes, until the liquid has just about been absorbed. Stir in the simmering stock, bring to a second boil, reduce the heat, cover, and simmer for 1 hour.

4. Stir in the broccoli and thyme and cook, uncovered, for another 10 minutes or until the liquid has just about been absorbed. Stir in the parsley, salt if necessary, pepper, and Parmesan and serve.

Baked Quinoa Casserole with Potatoes and Smoked Cheddar

Serves 6

Quinoa and potatoes both originated in Peru, so it seems logical to combine them in a rich, savory casserole. This comforting dish is great served hot from the oven, but I also like it cold.

> 1 tablespoon olive oil
> 2 leeks, white part only, cleaned and sliced
> 2 large garlic cloves, peeled and sliced
> 2 medium green bell peppers, diced
> 4 eggs
> ⅔ cup low-fat milk
> 1 cup quinoa, cooked (page 13)
> 4 ounces smoked Cheddar cheese, grated
>   (1 heaping cup)
> 1 pound unpeeled new potatoes, diced and
>   steamed until tender
> salt and freshly ground pepper to taste
> 1 teaspoon fresh thyme leaves or ½
>   teaspoon dried

1. Preheat the oven to 350 degrees. Oil a 2-quart casserole or soufflé dish.

2. Heat the olive oil in a heavy-bottomed nonstick skillet over medium-low heat and add the leeks. Cook, stirring, until they begin to soften, about 5 minutes, and add the garlic. Cook, stirring, for about 1 minute, then add the peppers. Cook over medium-low heat, stirring occasionally, for 5 to 10 minutes more, until the peppers are crisp-tender but still bright green. Remove from the heat.

3. Beat together the eggs and milk and stir in the quinoa, cheese, vegetables, salt, pepper, and thyme. Turn into the baking dish and bake 35 to 45 minutes, until the top is beginning to brown. Let the casserole sit for approximately 5 minutes before serving.

Spicy Zucchini and Bulgur Casserole

Serves 4

Mexican and Mediterranean flavors combine in this spicy, colorful combo.

1 cup medium-grind bulgur

boiling water to cover the bulgur

salt to taste

1 tablespoon olive oil

1 small onion, chopped

3 garlic cloves, minced or put through a press

2 pounds fresh or drained canned tomatoes, peeled, seeded, and chopped

2 tablespoons tomato paste

1 fresh serrano or jalapeño chili, seeded and minced

1 teaspoon chopped fresh rosemary or ½ teaspoon crumbled dried

freshly ground pepper to taste

2 tablespoons chopped cilantro

2 pounds zucchini, sliced ¼ inch thick

2 ounces Monterey Jack cheese, grated (½ cup)

1. Place the bulgur in a bowl and pour on boiling water to cover. Add about ¼ teaspoon of salt and stir together. Let sit until the bulgur is fluffy and has absorbed all the water, about 30 minutes.

2. Meanwhile, make the tomato sauce. Heat the oil in a heavy-bottomed saucepan over medium heat and add the onion and half the garlic. Sauté until the onion begins to soften, about 3 minutes, then add the tomatoes, tomato paste, remaining garlic, chili, rosemary, salt, and pepper. Bring to a boil, reduce the heat, cover, and simmer for 30 minutes, stirring often. Stir in the cilantro, taste, and adjust the seasonings.

>>>

3. While the tomato sauce is simmering, steam the zucchini for 5 minutes, until crisp-tender. Refresh under cold water and pat dry.

4. Oil a 3-quart baking dish. Preheat the oven to 350 degrees. Toss the bulgur with ½ cup of the tomato sauce and place in an even layer in the baking dish. Layer the zucchini on top of the bulgur and pour on the remaining tomato sauce. Sprinkle the cheese over the top. Bake for 30 to 40 minutes, until bubbling. Serve hot.

Kappamaki (Japanese Seaweed Rolls)

Makes 10 rolls, yielding 6 to 7 slices each

Here's a delicious way to impress your friends. The vegetarian sushi rolls we are used to eating only in restaurants are quite easy to make at home. You will need a bamboo rolling mat, pickled ginger, and wasabi, all available in Japanese food stores.

> 2 cups Italian Arborio rice
> 3 cups water
> ¼ cup rice vinegar
> 1 tablespoon sugar
> 2 teaspoons salt
> 10 sheets nori seaweed
> about 5 teaspoons wasabi (Japanese horseradish)
> 1 European cucumber, peeled, seeded, and cut in thin strips
> about ¾ cup pickled ginger to taste
> ½ cup water mixed with 1 tablespoon rice vinegar for dipping spoons and hands

1. Make the rice. Place in a colander in a bowl under cold running water for 15 minutes, or soak the rice for 15 minutes in a bowl of water. Drain and place in a medium-size, heavy-bottomed saucepan with the 3 cups water. Bring to

a boil and cover. Reduce the heat to medium and cook for 5 minutes, then reduce to very low and cook 6 to 10 minutes, until the water is absorbed and you hear the rice beginning to crackle on the bottom of the pan. Remove from the heat and let sit without removing the lid for 15 minutes.

2. Meanwhile, combine the vinegar, sugar, and salt in a saucepan. Heat through, stirring, until the sugar is dissolved. Allow to cool.

3. Transfer the rice to a bowl and, using one or two wooden spoons or paddles, whichever is easiest for you, gradually fold in the vinegar combination, a spoonful at a time. Dip the spoons or paddles into the water-vinegar mixture every so often so that the rice doesn't stick.

4. Toast the sheets of nori by fanning them over an open flame or a hot burner just until bright green (this happens in seconds). Position your bamboo mat so that it rolls away from you. Place the nori on the mat, shiny side down. Moisten your hands and a measuring spoon with the vinegar water and place 3 heaping tablespoons of the rice in the center of the nori. Spread evenly over the seaweed. It should be about ¼ to ½ inch thick and won't cover the entire sheet. Leave a margin of at least 1 inch at the top and bottom. Spread ¼ to ½ teaspoon of wasabi to taste down the middle of the rice, then add a layer of ginger and a layer of cucumber, about 4 strips thick.

5. To roll, fold the bamboo mat up at the middle to enclose the filling at the center of the nori. Press the mat around the nori and hold it firmly for about 30 seconds to shape it. Moisten the top edge of the nori with vinegar water and continue rolling up to seal. Remove the bamboo mat and place the roll on a cutting board, seam side down. Using a sharp, wet knife and a firm downward motion (do not saw), slice off the edges and slice the roll into ¾- to 1-inch rounds. Place the rolls on a wooden board or a plate, rice side up, and serve.

Note: For added protein, add strips of omelet to each roll. Make a thin omelet, using 2 eggs only, in a 10- or 12-inch omelet pan and cut into strips. Lay the strips on the rice, top with the cucumber and ginger and roll up.

Basmati Rice Pilaf with Indian Spices and Raita

Basmati rice is incredibly fragrant and goes beautifully with subtle Indian spices. This delicately flavored pilaf really comes to life when you add the minty raita.

For the Pilaf:
2 cups basmati rice
2 tablespoons canola oil
1 medium onion, chopped
2 garlic cloves, minced or put through a
    press
8 green cardamom pods
1 teaspoon crushed coriander seeds
1 cinnamon stick, 3 inches long
8 whole cloves
½ teaspoon powdered ginger
1 quart cold water
1 bay leaf
¾ to 1 teaspoon salt to taste
2 pounds (unshelled) fresh green peas, or 2
    cups defrosted frozen
freshly ground pepper

For the Raita:
2 cups plain low-fat yogurt
1 medium-size cucumber or ½ long
    European cucumber, peeled, seeded, and
    minced

2 to 3 tablespoons chopped fresh mint to
   taste
¾ teaspoon ground roasted cumin
¼ teaspoon chili powder
salt and freshly ground pepper to taste

1. Wash the rice thoroughly in several rinses of cold water. Soak in cold water for 30 minutes. Drain.

2. Heat 1 tablespoon of the oil in a large heavy-bottomed nonstick lidded skillet over medium heat and add the onion. Cook, stirring, until the onion is tender, about 5 minutes. Add the garlic and sauté for 30 seconds, then add another tablespoon of oil if necessary and the spices. Sauté another 30 seconds to a minute and stir in the rice. Continue to sauté, stirring, over medium heat for about 2 minutes, until the rice is translucent and beginning to brown.

3. Add the water, bay leaf, and salt. Bring to a boil, stirring, reduce the heat, and partially cover. Simmer 10 minutes, until most of the water has evaporated and small steam holes cover the surface of the rice.

4. Add the peas to the surface of the rice without stirring, cover tightly, and simmer another 5 minutes over very low heat. Turn off the heat and let sit 5 to 10 minutes without disturbing.

5. Meanwhile, make the raita. Beat the yogurt in a bowl with a whisk and mix in the remaining ingredients.

6. Uncover the pilaf, adjust salt, and stir in lots of freshly ground pepper. Turn the pilaf out onto a warm platter and pour half the raita over the top. Serve, passing the remaining raita.

METRIC CONVERSION CHART

CONVERSIONS OF OUNCES TO GRAMS

Ounces (oz)	Grams (g)
1 oz	30 g*
2 oz	60 g
3 oz	85 g
4 oz	115 g
5 oz	140 g
6 oz	180 g
7 oz	200 g
8 oz	225 g
9 oz	250 g
10 oz	285 g
11 oz	300 g
12 oz	340 g
13 oz	370 g
14 oz	400 g
15 oz	425 g
16 oz	450 g
20 oz	570 g
24 oz	680 g
28 oz	790 g
32 oz	900 g

*Approximate. To convert ounces to grams, multiply number of ounces by 28.35.

CONVERSIONS OF FAHRENHEIT TO CELSIUS

Fahrenheit	Celsius
170°F	77°C*
180°F	82°C
190°F	88°C
200°F	95°C
225°F	110°C
250°F	120°C
300°F	150°C
325°F	165°C
350°F	180°C
375°F	190°C
400°F	205°C
425°F	220°C
450°F	230°C
475°F	245°C
500°F	260°C
525°F	275°C
550°F	290°C

*Approximate. To convert Fahrenheit to Celsius, subtract 32, multiply by 5, then divide by 9.

CONVERSIONS OF POUNDS TO GRAMS AND KILOGRAMS

Pounds (lb)	Grams (g); kilograms (kg)
1 lb	450 g*
1¼ lb	565 g
1½ lb	675 g
1¾ lb	800 g
2 lb	900 g
2½ lb	1,125 g; 1¼ kg
3 lb	1,350 g
3½ lb	1,500 g; 1½ kg
4 lb	1,800 g
4½ lb	2 kg
5 lb	2¼ kg
5½ lb	2½ kg
6 lb	2¾ kg
6½ lb	3 kg
7 lb	3¼ kg
7½ lb	3½ kg
8 lb	3¾ kg
9 lb	4 kg
10 lb	4½ kg

*Approximate. To convert pounds into kilograms, multiply number of pounds by 453.6.

CONVERSIONS OF QUARTS TO LITERS

Quarts (qt)	Liters (L)
1 qt	1 L*
1½ qt	1½ L
2 qt	2 L
2½ qt	2½ L
3 qt	2¾ L
4 qt	3¾ L
5 qt	4¾ L
6 qt	5½ L
7 qt	6½ L
8 qt	7½ L
9 qt	8½ L
10 qt	9½ L

*Approximate. To convert quarts to liters, multiply number of quarts by 0.95.